GLADIATORS

FIGHTING to the DEATH

Gareth Stevens
Publishing

Alix Wood

Please visit our website, **www.garethstevens.com**. For a free color catalog of all our high-quality books, call toll free 1-800-542-2595 or fax 1-877-542-2596

Library of Congress Cataloging-in-Publication Data

Wood, Alix.
Gladiators: fighting to the death / by Alix Wood.
 p. cm. — (Why'd they do that? strange customs of the past)
Includes index.
ISBN 978-1-4339-9581-1 (pbk.)
ISBN 978-1-4339-9582-8 (6-pack)
ISBN 978-1-4339-9580-4 (library binding)
1. Gladiators—Rome—Juvenile literature. 2. Rome—Civilization—Juvenile literature. I. Wood, Alix. II. Title.
GV35.W66 2014
796.8—dc23

First Edition

Published in 2014 by
Gareth Stevens Publishing
111 East 14th Street, Suite 349
New York, NY 10003

Produced for Gareth Stevens by Alix Wood Books
Designed and illustrated by Alix Wood
Picture and content research: Kevin Wood
Editor: Eloise Macgregor

Photo credits:
Cover © Nejron Photo/Fotolia and © Olga Beregelia/Fotolia; 1 © Slaweek/Fotolia; 7 top © Dorieo/Ashmoleum Museum; 9 top © Jean-Pierre Dalbéra; 13 bottom © British Museum; 16 bottom © Chateau de Boudry; 19 top © Matthias Kabel; 19 bottom © Shakko; 21 top © Robert Schediwy; 23 bottom Raul654/Phoenix Art Museum; 24 bottom © Yomangani; 26 © Bureau L.A. Collection/Sygma/Corbis; 27 top © British Museum; 28 © CinemaPhoto/Corbis; 3, 4, 5, 6, 7 bottom, 9 middle and bottom left and right, 10, 11, 13 top, 17, 18, 20, 27 bottom © Shutterstock

Printed in the United States of America

CPSIA compliance information: Batch #CS13GS: For further information contact Gareth Stevens, New York, New York at 1-800-542-2595.

Contents

What Was a Gladiator?

Gladiators were fighters in ancient Rome who took part in organized fights for public entertainment. Roman gladiators were mostly slaves and prisoners, though some were paid. Some gladiators were free men who had sold themselves to a gladiator trainer because they needed the money. There were female gladiators, too, but most gladiators were men.

Gladiator fights were originally a custom of the Etruscan people, a civilization in Italy that existed before the Romans. When the master of the house died, his servants would fight to the death for the right to follow their master and provide help and company for him in the afterlife.

The first gladiatorial games in Rome were put on in honor of Junius Brutus Pera when he died. Gladiatorial combat became a popular sport and fights began being held in huge arenas. As the games became popular, the emperor kept the best gladiators in **imperial** schools and put on the greatest shows. Gladiator contests made their owners wealthy, and gladiators could be sold or hired out to make money, too.

A map showing Italy as it is today, in red

REALLY?

The word "gladiator" comes from the Latin word *gladius* which means "sword," so a gladiator is literally a swordsman.

HONORED SLAVES

The position of the gladiator in Roman society was interesting. While Romans looked down on gladiators as slaves, they were also respected as talented and skilled fighters. Gladiators were paid well for their fights, and some eventually bought their way to freedom. Many gladiators became celebrities. Roman women, in particular, admired gladiators. Many gladiators worked as bodyguards after their career in the arena was over. Gladiators, being trained warriors, were potentially the most dangerous slaves!

Wealthy citizens hired gladiators as bodyguards.

Life As a Slave

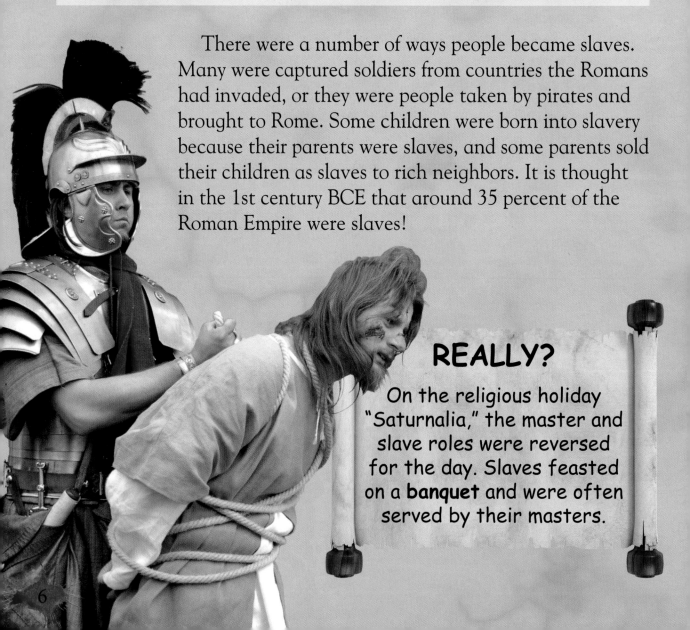

Being a slave in Roman times was a harsh life. Slaves did all the unpleasant jobs, like work underground in mines or in quarries breaking rock. Some worked on ships as galley slaves, chained below decks and made to row all day. Some slaves would work in the fields growing food. Becoming a gladiator wasn't the worst job for a slave.

There were a number of ways people became slaves. Many were captured soldiers from countries the Romans had invaded, or they were people taken by pirates and brought to Rome. Some children were born into slavery because their parents were slaves, and some parents sold their children as slaves to rich neighbors. It is thought in the 1st century BCE that around 35 percent of the Roman Empire were slaves!

REALLY?

On the religious holiday "Saturnalia," the master and slave roles were reversed for the day. Slaves feasted on a **banquet** and were often served by their masters.

THE SLAVE MARKET

Prisoners were taken to the slave-markets where they wore placards around their necks explaining their best and worst qualities. Sometimes slaves stood on revolving stands. If any information about the slaves was later found to be untrue, the buyer could take the seller to court. Prices varied with age and quality. The most valuable slaves fetched prices equivalent to thousands of today's dollars! You could buy all kinds of slaves from the market. Greek slaves were often highly educated and could be employed as doctors or teachers.

A relief showing a Roman soldier leading captives in chains

As more Roman men went off with the army to war, there were fewer men available to work the fields. Demand for slaves grew. Slave traders would follow the Roman army abroad on their **campaigns**. After a battle they would buy the defeated soldiers and their families, and then arrange for them to be sent back to Rome and elsewhere.

Only about half the gladiators who fought in Roman arenas were slaves. Some were ex-soldiers. Some were people who needed to pay off debts. Gladiators were allowed to keep their prize money and might be paid for each fight. The most successful gladiators were treated like modern-day pop stars. Some **volunteers** might have been trying to avoid military service. A volunteer gladiator signed up for three years, while military service was 20–25 years.

Gladiator School

Gladiators went to school to learn how to fight. People paid an entrance fee to watch gladiators training. The gladiator school was surrounded by fences and locked, guarded gates. There was no escape. The trainee gladiator's only hope was to learn how to fight well, so they could survive in the arena.

Gladiators were trained by a *lanista* which means "butcher"! A lanista was a retired gladiator. He would have survived many tough contests in the arena. His job was to get the new gladiators into shape and teach them the skills they would need to entertain the crowds in the arena. Hopefully, that would mean they would live to fight another day.

If the gladiators weren't well-prepared, the trainer would lose money. Wealthy Romans **invested** in the gladiator schools if they were successful, and this money paid the lanista's wages. Although a trainer may not have been the young gladiator's best friend, he had his best interests at heart—learning how to survive in the arena!

Lanistas were tough men. It was wise to listen to what they said!

8

A model of ancient Rome

Colosseum

Ludus Magnus

REALLY?

There were four gladiator schools in Rome. The largest was called the Ludus Magnus which means "big training ground." It had its own small arena and seated around 3,000 spectators. There was only one way out of this gladiator school—it was connected to the Colosseum arena by an underground tunnel!

SCHOOL FOOD

School food sometimes doesn't taste too good. Gladiator school food was very boring. Every day they would eat beans, barley, and porridge. As an extra body-building treat, they would get a spoonful or two of ash! Gladiators were fed so much barley they were called *hordearii*, which means "barley men." The porridge did help build up muscle, and the calcium in the ash was good for their bones.

Today's Menu

Starter
BARLEY

Main Course
PORRIDGE

Dessert
ASH

Yum!

In Training

New recruits were assessed by the lanista and by a doctor when they first arrived at gladiator school. They would check if they were physically suitable to become a gladiator. When gladiators first joined the school, they were ranked *novicius* which means "new." When they had completed their initial training and were ready to fight in the arena, they were called *tirones gladiatores* or "tiros." We still use the word "tyro" today to mean beginner. Gladiators who survived their first fight were known as *veteranus* or "**veterans**."

Gladiator training focused on the different fighting styles and weapons needed by specific types of gladiators. Gladiators who fought in heavy armor were generally stronger and slower than lightly-armed gladiators. The different types of gladiators needed customized training depending on their armor, weapons, and fighting techniques. Weapons included swords, spears, **tridents** and nets, and bows and arrows.

Gladiators had a ranking system. They trained using a pole called a *palus* buried in the ground. There were several poles in the training area. Gladiators that used the *primus palus*, meaning "first pole," were the best fighters. The second best used the *secundus palus* and so on down the rankings.

*Training included climbing ropes, throwing the **discus**, lifting rocks, or practicing with a spear.*

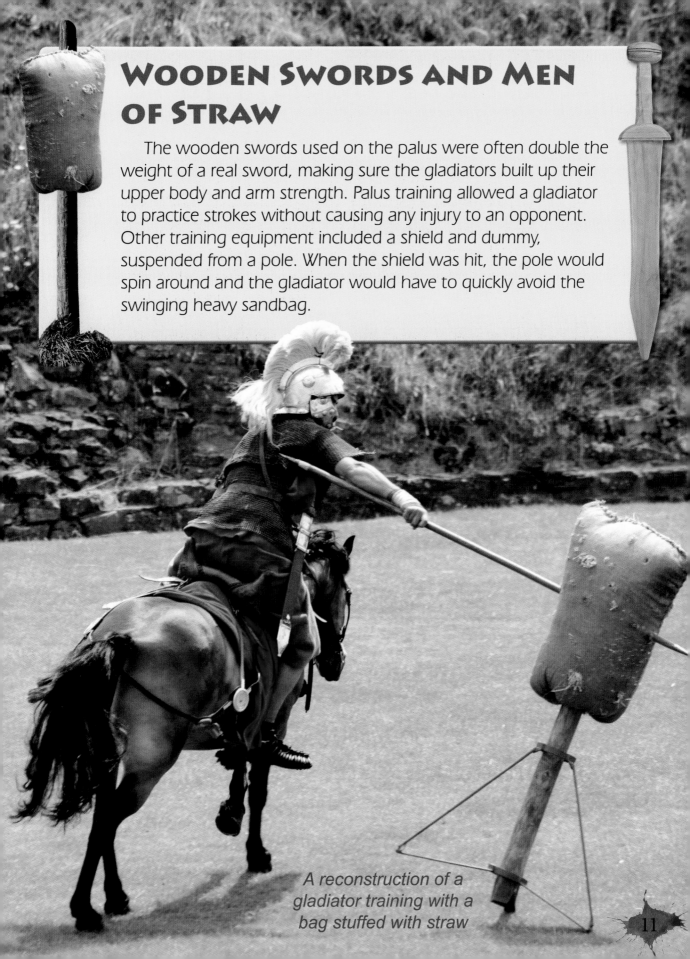

WOODEN SWORDS AND MEN OF STRAW

The wooden swords used on the palus were often double the weight of a real sword, making sure the gladiators built up their upper body and arm strength. Palus training allowed a gladiator to practice strokes without causing any injury to an opponent. Other training equipment included a shield and dummy, suspended from a pole. When the shield was hit, the pole would spin around and the gladiator would have to quickly avoid the swinging heavy sandbag.

A reconstruction of a gladiator training with a bag stuffed with straw

Gladiator Clothing

Gladiators often wore costumes and armor that mimicked mythical figures or Rome's past enemies. The costumes were part of the spectacle of the arena and could be quite elaborate. Different styles of gladiator would carry specific weapons for their type, too.

Gladiators would wear a simple tunic in the barracks, and then dress up for the arena. Information from statues and mosaics of gladiators can show us what they wore.

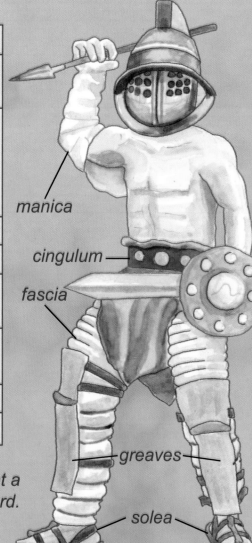

manica	Protective arm wraps
galerus	Left shoulder guard, worn by net and lasso fighters
greaves	Shin guards worn on the left or both legs. They were knee-high or mid-thigh depending on the size of the shield used
thorax	A metal breastplate
fascia	Protective leg padding
cingulum	A wide belt, often with hanging studded leather straps
tunica	A thigh-length sleeveless garment, fastened with a belt
caliga	Heavy hob-nailed military boot
solea	Gladiators' sandals

A gladiator called a hoplomachus *often fought a* murmillo. *He carried a spear and a short sword.*

REALLY?

There were laws in Rome which governed what people were allowed to wear. For instance, only Roman citizens were allowed to wear the toga (pictured right). The emperor was the only person allowed to wear a purple toga. Even though gladiators could be wealthy, they were slaves and could only buy clothes like tunics and cloaks.

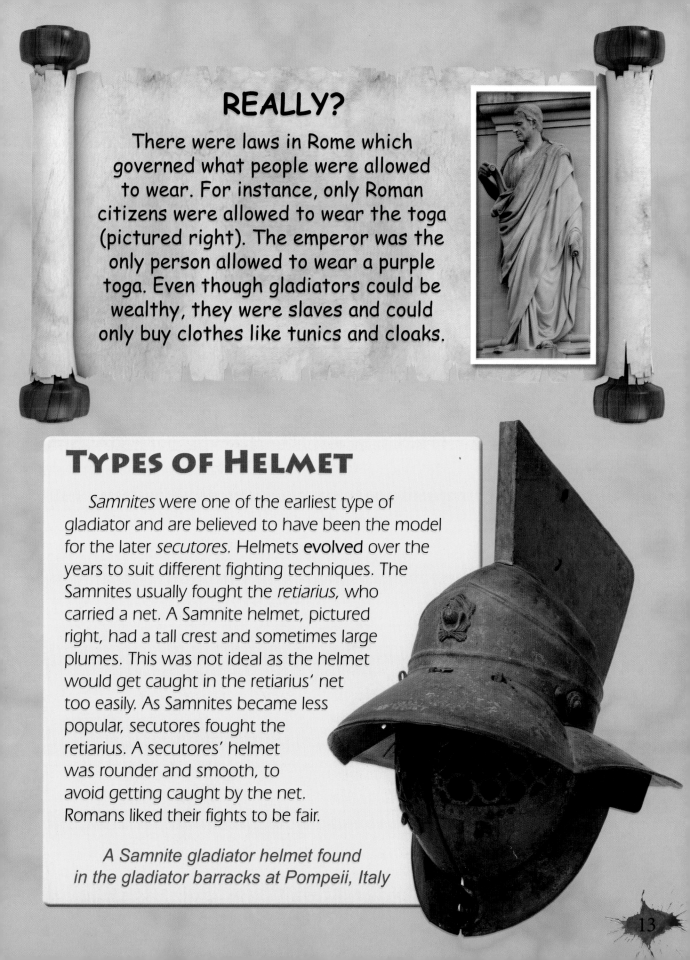

TYPES OF HELMET

Samnites were one of the earliest type of gladiator and are believed to have been the model for the later *secutores*. Helmets **evolved** over the years to suit different fighting techniques. The Samnites usually fought the *retiarius*, who carried a net. A Samnite helmet, pictured right, had a tall crest and sometimes large plumes. This was not ideal as the helmet would get caught in the retiarius' net too easily. As Samnites became less popular, secutores fought the retiarius. A secutores' helmet was rounder and smooth, to avoid getting caught by the net. Romans liked their fights to be fair.

A Samnite gladiator helmet found in the gladiator barracks at Pompeii, Italy

Types of Gladiator

During gladiator training, each pupil would be assigned to a particular *doctores*. A doctores is a trainer in a type of fighting. A trainer who trained a type of gladiator called a retiarius would be called *doctores retiarii* and one who trained secutores would be a *doctores secutorum*. There were many different types of gladiator.

One of the rules of the arena was that a fight should be as evenly matched as possible. If a gladiator didn't wear much armor, then his weapons needed to be more dangerous than those of his more protected opponent. Heavy armor would make a gladiator slow, and so it would become a fair fight. Gladiators who were similarly armed, therefore, rarely competed against one another. Most contests, in fact, seem to have been between the lightly armed *thraex* or retiarius against their more heavily armed adversaries.

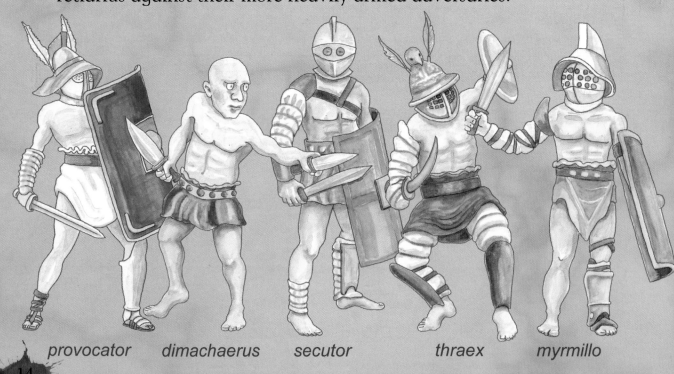

provocator   dimachaerus   secutor   thraex   myrmillo

During training, members of the same fighting-style bonded together. It was often a gladiator's fellows who would pay for his tombstone. It was fortunate that only some fighting styles had to fight each other to the death.

REALLY?

Left-handed gladiators were advertised as an interesting rarity; it gave them advantage over most opponents and produced an unusual contest.

WHO FIGHTS WHO?

Here are some typical gladiator pairings;

hoplomachus vs myrmillo
hoplomachus vs thraex
myrmillo vs thraex
retiarius vs myrmilllo
retiarius vs secutor
essedarius vs essedarius
provocator vs provocator

Greek pottery from the British Museum showing a hoplomachus (left) fighting a thraex (right)

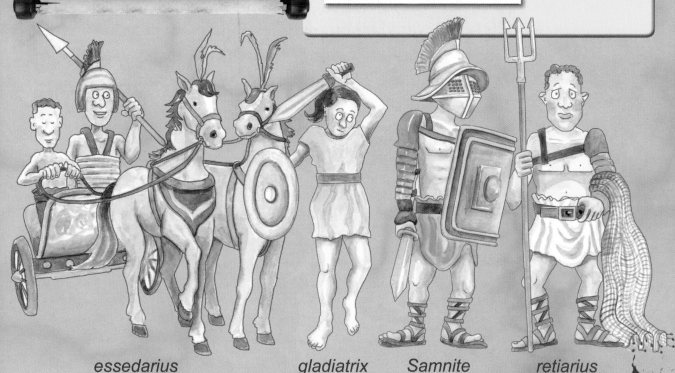

essedarius   *gladiatrix*   *Samnite*   *retiarius*

The Games Commence!

Gladiator games were expensive to organize. The person responsible for putting on the games was called the *editor*. He would hire a lanista to help him. They would agree costs such as how much the editor should pay the lanista if one of his gladiators was killed. Before the games, the lanista would send slaves to paint signs on the walls advertising the contests. A program was prepared for the day, too, with the names, types, and match records of gladiator pairs and their order of appearance. This information was useful to gamblers.

The day before the gladiatorial games, a public banquet was held for the gladiators called the *coena libera*. The feast was a way for citizens to pay tribute to the fighters for sacrificing their lives for their entertainment. It also acted as advertising for the games. Whatever the reasons, it must have been a welcome meal after all that barley! The gladiators were all aware it could be their last meal. Some would eat well, but others would probably have no appetite at all, terrified at the prospect of what was to come.

*A **mosaic** of a Roman banquet*

THE SEATING PLAN

All gladiator arenas had the same basic shape and layout. They were oval, with blocks of seating rising up on all sides. They had an entrance at each end. The gladiators came out of one entrance. The other entrance was for servants and carrying out dead gladiators. The shady seats on the south side were for the more important citizens.

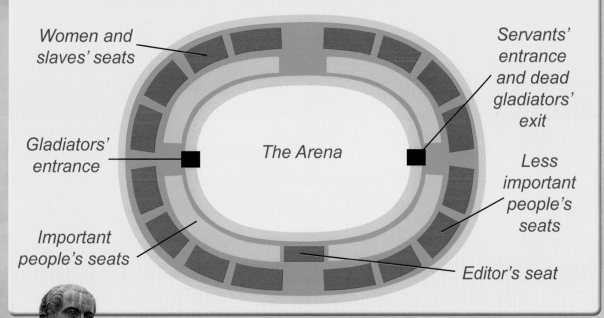

Women and slaves' seats

Servants' entrance and dead gladiators' exit

Gladiators' entrance

The Arena

Less important people's seats

Important people's seats

Editor's seat

The editor of the games received **adulation** if his spectacle was great entertainment. Editors were often politicians who staged the games to win popularity and votes. Julius Caesar, who became emperor of Rome, was editor of a great games early in his career. However, Emperor Vitellius was murdered by a mob after hosting a poor contest! Rich men who lent money to the editor would get the best seats in the arena. Citizens known to be voting for an opponent would be turned away from the games.

A statue of Julius Caesar

What's on the Bill?

On the day of the games, the spectacle would begin with a parade. The editor would parade around the arena, often in a chariot, along with the gladiators and with musicians playing a fanfare. Slaves would follow holding the gladiators' costumes. Statues of the gods were carried in to witness the proceedings, followed by a **scribe** to record the outcome, and a man carrying the palm branch used to honor the victors.

The editor or an honored guest would check the gladiators' weapons in a ceremony called *probatio armorum*. This process could be as inventive, varied, and novel as the editor could afford. Sometimes the swords were tested by slicing up vegetables and the armor was tested by being hit by clubs! Sometimes elaborately decorated **armatures** were used.

PROGRAM OF EVENTS

PARADE

PROBATIO ARMORUM

MUSICIANS

WOODEN SWORD FIGHTS

GLADIATOR CONTESTS

LUNCH AND EXECUTION OF CRIMINALS

SEA BATTLE

WILD BEASTS

Gladiators had umpires! They are often shown in the background in mosaics. The rules of gladiatorial combat are unknown, but the umpire's presence suggests that the rules were complex and **contentious**.

A reconstruction of a gladiator fight between two provocatores, with umpire

The mosaic on the right shows entertainment from a typical gladiatorial games. Pictured from the top are musicians, gladiator fights, criminal executions by animals, and animal hunts and fights. The musical instruments are typical of those used at the games. The woman seated in the top panel is playing a water organ. The two men next to her are playing curved instruments called *cornua*. The mosaic is from a Roman seaside villa in Zliten, Libya.

19

A Gladiator Arena

The first gladiator contests were held in marketplaces or forums. The earliest known Roman **amphitheater** was built at Pompeii around 70 BCE. The first in the city of Rome was an extraordinary wooden amphitheater built for the games of Gaius Scribonius Curio in 53 BCE. Two wooden semicircular theaters were rotated towards each other to form one circular amphitheater, while spectators were still seated in the two halves!

When the first part-stone amphitheater in Rome burned down, Emperor Vespasian began its replacement, the Colosseum, below. The Colosseum seated 50,000 spectators. It was completed in the reign of Emperor Titus, and his **inaugural** games lasted 100 days! It was known as the Colosseum as it was built next to a large statue of Nero called the "Colossus."

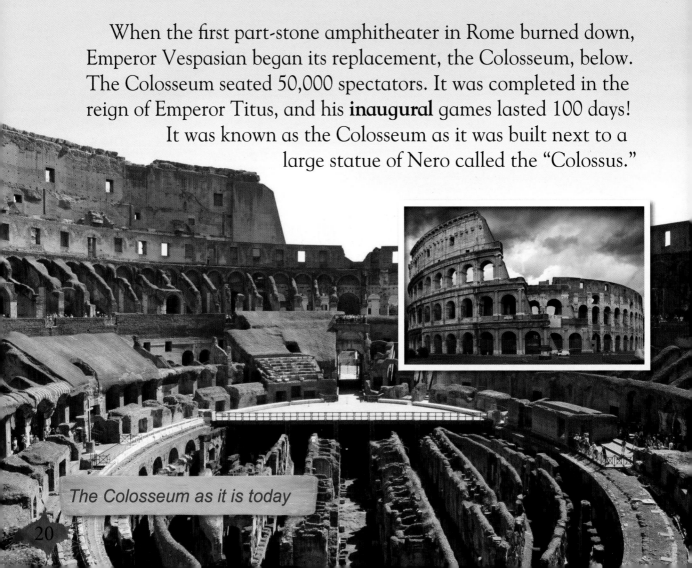

The Colosseum as it is today

Not all amphitheaters are as well preserved as the Colosseum. Many were dismantled for building material. Others were transformed into fortified settlements like this one at Arles, France. Engraving by J.B. Guibert, 18th century.

REALLY?

The word *arena* is Latin for "sanded area." Arenas had sandy floors to soak up the blood. The sand was about 6 inches (15 cm) deep and covered a wooden floor. The sand had to be constantly replaced as more blood was spilled.

TUNNELS UNDER THE ARENA

The Colosseum had a network of underground passages where the gladiators and animals were kept before the games. There were 36 trapdoors in the wooden floor of the arena. During the games, scenery, gladiators, and exotic wild animals would magically appear through these trapdoors. The area beneath the Colosseum was called the *hypogeum* and was a two-level network of tunnels and 32 animal pens. Large animals such as elephants and hippopotamus were put on strong hinged platforms which could also be hoisted up to the arena.

A Gladiator Contest

Entering the arena must have been terrifying. The crowd would have been vast and noisy. Gladiators would sometimes fight with wooden swords to warm up before their fight. Then music would sound, and they would be given their real weapons.

It was important to put on a good show for the crowd. They would be more likely to spare a gladiator who had fought well and entertained them. If a gladiator did not fight to his trainer's satisfaction, the lanista would send a slave into the arena to whip the gladiator or prod them with a hot poker. Roman gladiators were expected to die with dignity, honor, and no complaint. They were never allowed to show fear.

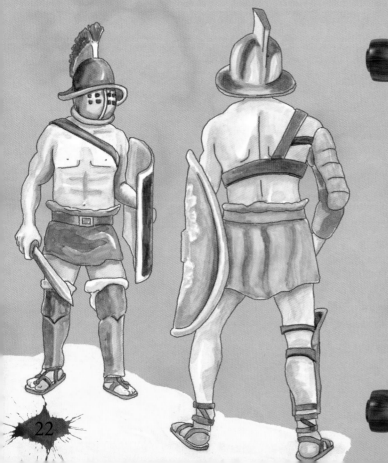

REALLY?

If any gladiators sentenced to death were dying but still alive, a man dressed as Charon would come over and finish them off with a double-headed hammer. Charon was a mythical figure who ferried souls to the underworld.

GENEROUS EMPEROR

If a gladiator lost his contest in Rome, he could appeal to the emperor to save him by raising one finger on his left hand. The emperor would often ask the crowd if he should be spared. If the crowd made a stabbing motion with their thumbs down, the defeated gladiator must die. If not, he was spared. Emperor Titus is said to have thrown wooden balls into the crowd from his seat. Written on the balls was a description of a gift, such as food, clothing, slaves, or horses. Anyone who caught a ball could hand it to an official who would give them the named gift in return!

Fights were rarely to the death as gladiators were valuable to their owners and popular with the public. If a gladiator died, the lanista charged the editor up to a hundred times the cost of a gladiator who survived. It was therefore expensive for editors to supply the bloodshed that audiences demanded. If the emperor was not at the games, it was the editor who decided the fate of the victim. He would probably be more likely to grant mercy!

The crowd is signaling with their thumbs that they want the defeated gladiator to die.

23

Sea Battles

Sea battles, called *naumachiae*, took place on a man-made lake beside the river Tiber in Rome. The sea battles were based on real battles fought between the Greeks and the Egyptians or Persians years before. The gladiators would dress in those countries' costumes. The battle was then fought for real, and would not always end the same way the actual battle had done.

The gladiators often used small battleships called biremes and triremes. A bireme had two decks of oars. It was about 80 feet (24 m) long and needed 120 rowers. The trireme was the same length, but had three tiers of oarsmen and a large square sail. The gladiators would fire burning arrows at the enemy ships, and then try to board them. One record says at Emperor Augustus's sea battle, a walled island was built in the middle of a lake with a monument on it and was connected to the shore by a bridge.

AMPHITHEATER SEA BATTLES

Sea battles in amphitheaters were probably only performed in shallow water. The technicalities of filling and draining the space would have been very awkward. It is possible they used stage props to look like ships, and they wouldn't have actually floated. It still must have been quite a spectacle though.

An old engraving of a sea battle by an unknown artist

Sea battles were bloodier than gladiatorial combat. Gladiator contests were usually one on one and often did not end in death. A sea battle involved two armies and many would die. Emperor Claudius's naumachia used prisoners who had been condemned to death. Before the battle, the prisoners were made to salute the emperor with the phrase *morituri te salutant* which means "those who are about to die salute you."

In smaller amphitheaters, the boats would be smaller so they could turn easily in the small area.

REALLY?

When the Colosseum was first built, it was used for sea battles. It was flooded with water using special pipes that could drain the water away again at the end of the battle. When the underground tunnels were built, this was no longer possible.

Fighting Wild Beasts

Wild animal hunts were a spectator favorite at the games. The arena would be transformed into a park, with trees, rocks, and wild animals appearing out of the trapdoors in the floor. *Venatores* were trained to hunt animals such as deer, wild boar, or wolves. *Bestiarii* fought more exotic wild animals, like tigers and elephants.

The venatores were trained at a special training school called the *ludus matutinus* which means "morning school," as animal shows were initially morning events at the Colosseum. The ludus matutinus was established by the Emperor Domitian who was a great hunter.

The Bestiarii schools were called the *scholae bestiarum* or the *bestiariorum*. Both slaves and volunteers were trained to fight with wild beasts. They used weapons such as nets, arrows, and spears. Condemned criminals would also be put in the arena to face exotic wild animals, usually with no weapons.

A still from the film Gladiator, *showing a tiger in the arena*

REALLY?

During the first games at the Colosseum, over 9,000 wild animals were slaughtered! At a games in 240 AD, 2,000 gladiators, 70 lions, 40 wild horses, 30 elephants, 30 leopards, 20 wild asses, 19 giraffes, 10 antelopes, 10 hyenas, 10 tigers, 1 hippopotamus, and 1 rhinoceros were slaughtered. So many wild animals were killed in Roman arenas that some exotic animals became virtually extinct.

A marble relief from the British Museum shows a fight between a venator and a lion.

TIDYING UP THE ARENA

At the end of the games, slaves would remove the bodies of gladiators, sometimes with dignity, but sometimes they were dragged from the arena using hooks. In the morgue, bodies were stripped of valuable armor, which was given back to the lanista. To ensure there had not been any **match-fixing**, and the gladiator was really dead, they would cut his throat! Gladiators were buried in their own separate cemeteries. Even in death, gladiators never escaped the social stigma of their profession.

The Death of a Gladiator *engraving by Peyns from a picture by Marco Landuchchi*

Famous Gladiators

Some gladiators achieved fame during their careers. Graffiti at the gladiator school at Pompeii reads "Celadus the Thracian makes the girls sigh," although it may well have been written by Celadus himself! The Emperor Commodus often fought in the arena as a secutor. He fought gladiators as well as wild animals. Perhaps the most famous gladiator of all was Spartacus.

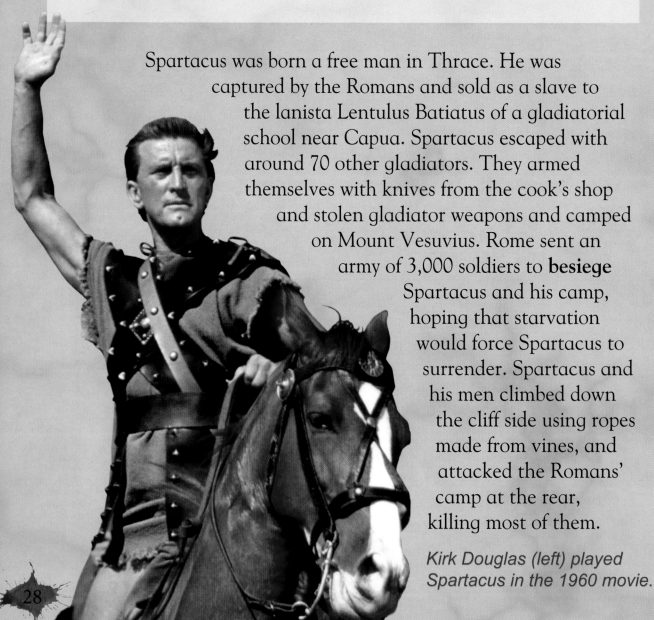

Spartacus was born a free man in Thrace. He was captured by the Romans and sold as a slave to the lanista Lentulus Batiatus of a gladiatorial school near Capua. Spartacus escaped with around 70 other gladiators. They armed themselves with knives from the cook's shop and stolen gladiator weapons and camped on Mount Vesuvius. Rome sent an army of 3,000 soldiers to **besiege** Spartacus and his camp, hoping that starvation would force Spartacus to surrender. Spartacus and his men climbed down the cliff side using ropes made from vines, and attacked the Romans' camp at the rear, killing most of them.

Kirk Douglas (left) played Spartacus in the 1960 movie.

Rome tried again. This time they sent 6,000 men. Spartacus won that battle as well. Many other slaves ran away to join him and his followers swelled from 70 to around 90,000 people! Spartacus and his followers were hunted for two years. They defeated every effort to capture them. When Rome finally caught up with him, they killed Spartacus and everyone with him.

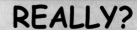

REALLY?

Spartacus was killed, but his body was never found. It is said that 6,000 survivors of the revolt captured by the Roman legions were crucified, lining the Appian Way, the main route from Rome to Capua, as a warning to other slaves.

KEEPING SCORE

Apart from the tombstones of the gladiators, graffiti scratched on walls giving a tally of individual gladiators' records are the most detailed sources that modern historians have for the careers of these ancient fighters. These drawings found on the podium of a tomb at Pompeii records the career of Marcus Attilius. As a tiro, he beat the experienced Hilarus, even though Hilarus had won a wreath 13 times. Wreaths were awarded to victors at gladiator games. Attilius then defeated Lucius Raecius Felix, who had won 12 wreaths. Both Hilarus and Raecius must have fought well against Attilius, as each of them was granted a **reprieve**.

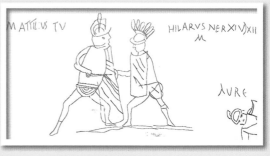

Drawings of the Marcus Attilius graffiti. V means vicit or victorious, M means missus or defeated but spared, P means perit or dead

Glossary

adulation
Admiration and praise.

amphitheater
A building with seats rising in curved rows around an open space on which games and shows take place.

armatures
Frameworks serving as the supporting cores for material used to make a sculpture.

banquet
A formal dinner for many people often in honor of someone.

besiege
To surround with armed forces for the purpose of capturing.

campaigns
A series of military operations in a particular area or for a particular purpose as part of a war.

contentious
Involving or likely to cause contention; controversial.

discus
A heavy disk that is hurled for distance.

evolved
Changed and developed from something else.

imperial
Relating to an empire or an emperor.

inaugural
Marking a celebration of an opening or beginning.

invest
To lay out money so as to return a profit.

match-fixing
Pre-determining who wins a match by cheating.

mosaic
A decoration made of small pieces of tile of different colors to make pictures or patterns.

reprieve
An escape, either permanently or temporarily, from expected punishment or consequences.

scribe
An official writer of documents.

trident
A spear with three prongs.

veterans
People who have had much experience.

volunteers
Persons doing something of their own free will.

For More Information
Books

Lacey, Minna. *Gladiators.* Usborne Books, 2006.

Malam, John. *You Wouldn't Want to Be a Roman Gladiator.* Franklin Watts, 2013.

Matthews, Rupert. *100 Things You Should Know About Gladiators.* Mason Crest, 2011.

Websites

Gladiator: Dressed to Kill Game
http://www.bbc.co.uk/history/ancient/romans/launch_gms_gladiator.shtml
Dress a gladiator for battle in the Roman arena. The game teaches you what each type of gladiator wore into the arena.

Kidipede Ancient Rome
www.historyforkids.org/learn/romans/games/circus.htm/
Find out everything you need to know about ancient Rome and the gladiators.

Roman Empire and Colosseum
www.roman-colosseum.info/gladiators/
Facts, information, and details about the gladiators who fought to the death in the bloody arena of the Roman Colosseum.

Index